The Vimto® Cookbook

SERIOUSLY MIXED UP RECIPES

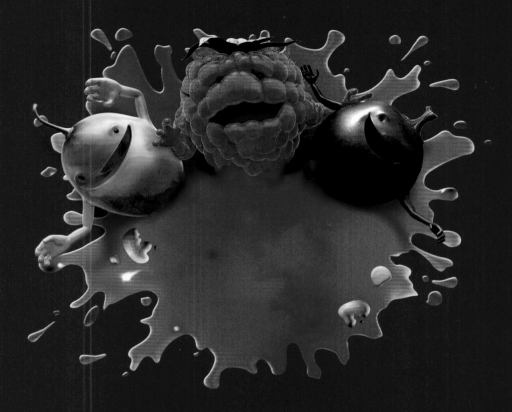

SERIOUSLY
MIXED UP RECIPES

PAUL HARTLEY AND DAVID CLARE

A.

First published in Great Britain in 2014
by Absolute Press,
an imprint of Bloomsbury Publishing Plc

Absolute Press
Scarborough House
29 James Street West
Bath BA1 2BT
Phone 44 (0) 1225 316013
Fax 44 (0) 1225 445836
E-mail office@absolutepress.co.uk
Website www.absolutepress.co.uk

Publisher Jon Croft
Commissioning Editor Meg Avent
Art Direction and Design Matt Inwood
Project Editor Alice Gibbs
Editor Annie Lee
Photography Mike Cooper
Food Styling Genevieve Taylor

ISBN 9781472905581

Printed and bound in China by C&C Printing.

A catalogue record of this book is available from the
British Library.

Bloomsbury Publishing Plc
50 Bedford Square
London WC1B 3DP
www.bloomsbury.com

Bloomsbury is a trademark of
Bloomsbury Publishing Plc

This book is produced under licence from Nichols Plc,
WA12 0HH; owner of the registered trademark Vimto®.

A note about the text
This book was set using Helvetica Neue and Pig.
Helvetica was designed in 1957 by Max Miedinger
of the Swiss-based Haas foundry. In the early 1980s,
Linotype redrew the entire Helvetica family.
The result was Helvetica Neue. The Pig font was
designed by Marcio Hirosse.

CONTENTS

PRESENTING...

THE VIMTO
RECIPE COLLECTION

VIMTO AND BLUEBERRY SMOOTHIE

PER PERSON

300ml natural yoghurt
3 tablespoons Vimto squash
1 teaspoon runny honey
a handful of fresh blueberries

Put all the ingredients into a blender and blitz.
If you are using a thick yoghurt you may need
to add a splash of water to get a good drinking
consistency.

Pour into a tall glass and serve with a straw.

IN THE
BEGINNING...

(John) Noel Nichols was born on December
28th 1883 in Blackburn, Lancashire. After
working as a stockbroker's clerk and a soap
factory manager, Noel decided to enter the
world of flavours, herbs and spices....

One giant leap towards Vimto! The creator of
what would become one of the most popular
soft drinks in the world first set up his small
wholesale druggist and herbalist business
in central Manchester. Surrounded by the
aroma of essences, herbs and spices, Noel
experimented with a range of flavoured fruit
squashes.

VIMTO AUTUMN CHUTNEY

MAKES ABOUT 6x500g JARS

3kg cooking apples, peeled, cored and
    roughly chopped
juice of 1 lemon
50ml Vimto squash
1 large onion, finely diced
450g sultanas
3 garlic cloves, finely diced
500ml malt vinegar
500ml cider vinegar
1.5kg demerara sugar
½ teaspoon ground cloves
2 teaspoons ground cinnamon
a 2cm piece of fresh ginger, finely diced
2 teaspoons salt

Put all the ingredients into a large heavy-based saucepan and heat gently, stirring until all the sugar has dissolved. Bring the mixture to the boil, then turn down to a very gentle simmer and cook for 1½–2 hours, stirring occasionally to make sure it doesn't stick to the pan.

Remove the pan from the heat. Put six glass jars (without lids) on to a baking tray and pop them into a hot oven for 5 minutes to sterilise them. Carefully ladle the chutney into the warm jars and as soon as you are able to handle them, pop the lids firmly on.

Label when cold and wait for at least a month before using. The chutney will keep for 6 months in a sealed jar; once opened, keep it in the fridge. Delicious with pork or gammon, and perfect for a lunchtime ploughman's.

BEETROOT AND GOAT'S CHEESE SALAD WITH VIMTO DRESSING

SERVES 4

2 large handfuls of mixed salad leaves, washed
150g goat's cheese
8 cooked baby beetroots (not in vinegar)
a handful of walnut pieces
a few basil leaves, torn

FOR THE DRESSING

3 tablespoons white wine vinegar
1½ teaspoons Vimto squash
3 tablespoons olive oil
1 teaspoon acacia honey
a squeeze of lime juice
salt and freshly ground black pepper

Put all the dressing ingredients into a clean jam jar, put the lid on securely and shake well to emulsify.

Scatter the salad leaves over four plates, then crumble the goat's cheese evenly over the leaves. Cut the beetroots into bite-size pieces and divide them between the plates. Add the walnuts, then the basil, and finally drizzle with the delicious Vimto dressing.

WHAT'S IN A NAME?

Did you know that Vimto was first registered as a medicine? In 1912 it was originally intended as a pick-me-up health tonic to give those who drank it 'vim', which means energy or power. So Noel Nichols called his new wonder invention Vim Tonic. The name Vimto came about from a snappy combination of the two words.

"I can't see my Diet Vimto!"

Left: a humorous showcard from 1987, advertising Diet Vimto, featuring one of the Roly Polys.

Right: a showcard from the 1950s, indicating how Vimto has always appealed to all generations.

FOR YOUNG AND OLD!

DEEP-FRIED BRIE WITH VIMTO AND REDCURRANT SAUCE

SERVES 6

FOR THE BRIE

600g Brie cheese
breadcrumbs
plain flour
2 eggs, beaten with a splash of milk
vegetable oil, for frying

FOR THE SAUCE

1 small onion
a little sunflower oil, for frying
450g redcurrants
100g soft brown sugar
200ml Vimto squash

Keep the Brie in the fridge until the very last minute.

Place some breadcrumbs, flour and the beaten egg mixture in three separate bowls. Remove the Brie from the fridge and trim off as much rind as possible. Cut the Brie into six wedges and dip them into the bowls in the following order: egg, flour, egg, breadcrumbs, making sure each time that they are completely covered. Put them back into the fridge to chill.

Finely dice the onion and fry in a little oil until translucent. Add the redcurrants, sugar, Vimto squash and 200ml of water and simmer gently until the mixture has the consistency of thick jam. Transfer to a jar or bowl and leave to cool.

When the sauce is cooled, it's time to cook the cheese.

Heat about 5cm of oil in a deep frying pan and carefully place the wedges of Brie in the very hot oil. When they are evenly golden brown on one side, turn them over and repeat. Remove from the pan and place on kitchen paper to drain.

Serve with the redcurrant sauce and a crisp side salad.

BABY BEETROOTS IN VIMTO JELLY

SERVES 6

4 leaves of gelatine
50ml Vimto squash
1 teaspoon balsamic vinegar
8 cooked baby beetroots
freshly ground black pepper

You will need a 500ml pudding bowl or similar sized mould.

Soak the gelatine leaves in cold water for 10 minutes.

Put the Vimto squash and balsamic vinegar into a small saucepan with 100ml of water and bring to the boil. Remove from the heat and add the gelatine a leaf at a time, so that it completely dissolves. Season with a good grind of pepper and stir, then set aside to cool a little.

Cut enough of the beetroot in half to line the bowl up to the rim, with the cut side against the sides, and put the rest into the middle. Pour in the jelly mixture and allow to cool completely. Cover with clingfilm and pop into the fridge to set.

When you are ready to eat, dip the bowl into hot water for a few seconds to loosen the jelly and turn it out on to a plate.

This is really good with cold cuts on Boxing Day.

A GLOBAL TONIC!

By the 1930s Noel Nichols was able to claim that Vimto was available from Peru to Albania. The drink was and still is hugely popular throughout the Middle East, Africa and further afield. Today, it is available in more than 70 countries!

PAN-FRIED PRAWNS WITH VIMTO AND SOY

SERVES 4 AS A STARTER

- 1 tablespoon Vimto squash
- 1 teaspoon dark soy sauce
- 2 teaspoons lime juice
- 2 tablespoons sweet chilli dipping sauce
- 1 teaspoon fish sauce
- 1 tablespoon runny honey
- ½ teaspoon Chinese five-spice
- 1 tablespoon sesame seeds
- 250g raw king prawns
- 4 iceberg lettuce leaves, to serve as shells

In a small bowl mix together the Vimto squash, soy sauce, lime juice, sweet chilli, fish sauce, honey and five-spice. Toast the sesame seeds in a small dry frying pan until golden and set aside.

Put a large frying pan or wok over a medium heat and pour in the spicy Vimto sauce. Add the prawns and cook for 3–4 minutes, moving them around in the sauce until they are pink and fully cooked.

Arrange the lettuce leaves on four warmed plates, divide the prawns and sauce between them, and sprinkle with the toasted sesame seeds.

THE VIMTO

DON'T MISS LOTS OF BUMPER FUN OFFERS INSIDE

MICK 'n MAX — THE NEW FUN COMIC 5p

MICK 'n MAX · FELIX THE FERRET

FIZZY LIZZY · NORMAN · SIDNEY 'n 'ARRY EDGEHOG

Comic-book Vimto from the 1980s.

MACKEREL WITH GOOSEBERRY SAUCE AND NEW POTATOES

SERVES 4

500g new potatoes
50g butter
300g gooseberries, topped and tailed
100ml Vimto squash
4 mackerel fillets
oil, for cooking
1 tablespoon chopped fresh parsley
salt and freshly ground black pepper

Boil the potatoes in plenty of salted water until they are tender and drop off when picked up with the tip of a knife.

Gently melt half the butter in a saucepan and add the gooseberries. Simmer gently until the fruit has softened, then add the Vimto squash and 100ml of water and continue simmering until you have the consistency of jam but with some of the fruit still intact.

Season the mackerel with salt and pepper and cook in a large frying pan with a hint of oil, skin side down first, for 2–3 minutes each side. Remove the fish from the pan and place on kitchen paper to drain and keep warm.

Drain the potatoes and put them back into the cooking pan. Place the pan back on a gentle heat and add the rest of the butter and the parsley. When the butter has melted, gently roll the potatoes around the pan until they are coated.

Serve the mackerel with some gooseberry sauce spooned over half the fish and with a side of buttery new potatoes.

SALMON CURED IN VIMTO AND DILL

SERVES 6-8 AS A STARTER

2 salmon fillets, skin on, 350–400g each
4 tablespoons Vimto squash
2 tablespoons Maldon sea salt
2 tablespoons chopped fresh dill

Lay one of the salmon fillets, skin side down, in a shallow dish and spoon over the Vimto squash. Sprinkle over all the sea salt, and finally press all the chopped dill over the salmon flesh. Now place the other fillet, flesh side down, on top. Cover with clingfilm, put a plate smaller than the dish on top, and weight down with some tins from the store cupboard. Put into the fridge for 3 days.

When ready to serve, remove the fish from the marinade, place on a wooden board and bring back to room temperature. Slice very thinly, and serve with brown bread and butter and a little horseradish mayonnaise.

CHICKEN KEBABS WITH THYME, MUSTARD AND VIMTO SAUCE

SERVES 2

2 chicken breasts
600ml chicken stock
1 teaspoon fresh thyme leaves
1 tablespoon Vimto squash
2 teaspoons runny honey
1 teaspoon wholegrain mustard
12 rashers of pancetta or smoked streaky
  bacon
vegetable oil, for frying
salt and freshly ground black pepper

You will need four metal or bamboo skewers (pre-soaked in water).

Put the chicken breasts into a saucepan with the chicken stock and poach over a gentle heat for 10–15 minutes, depending on size, until they are just cooked through and firm to the touch.

Put the thyme leaves, Vimto squash, honey and mustard into a small saucepan and mix together, then place on a medium heat and cook for a couple of minutes.

Take the chicken breasts out of the stock and place them on a board. As soon as they are cool enough to handle, cut each breast into 6 chunks. Season with salt and pepper and wrap each piece of chicken once round with a piece of pancetta. Assemble evenly on the skewers and brush with the thyme sauce.

Heat a little oil in a large frying pan and add the kebabs. Fry until the pancetta is crispy and golden, basting with the sauce as you go.

Serve with a crunchy salad and with any remaining sauce drizzled over the kebabs.

The first Vimto can was introduced in 1964, featuring the iconic stripe design which would go on to make the brand one of the most immediately recognisable brands of its time.

CHINESE CHICKEN AND EGG-FRIED RICE

SERVES 4

FOR THE CHINESE CHICKEN

2 chicken breasts
1 tablespoon hoisin sauce
1 tablespoon tomato ketchup
½ tablespoon sweet chilli sauce
3 tablespoons Vimto squash

FOR THE RICE

groundnut oil, for frying
a 2cm piece of fresh ginger, grated
2 spring onions, finely sliced
2 garlic cloves, finely chopped
200g cooked white long-grain rice (about 70g
    uncooked), left to cool
2 eggs, beaten
2 tablespoons Shaoxing rice wine
1 tablespoon rice wine vinegar
2 tablespoons soy sauce

Cut the chicken breasts into bite-size pieces and fry in a little hot oil in a frying pan until golden. Remove from the pan with a slotted spoon and set aside. Add the remaining chicken ingredients to the pan along with 4 tablespoons of water, and mix well. Return the chicken to the sauce and simmer gently for 8–10 minutes, or until tender and cooked through.

Heat a little oil in a separate frying pan or wok and add the ginger, spring onions and garlic. Fry gently for a couple of minutes, being careful not to burn the garlic. Add the cold rice and stir quickly until coated in the oil.

Make a well in the centre of the rice and add the beaten eggs. Stir quickly with chopsticks to create a scrambled-egg-like mixture in the middle of the pan. Once the egg has solidified, stir it into the rice until evenly distributed.

Add the rice wine, rice wine vinegar and soy sauce, to taste.

Serve the rice with the chicken and sauce.

A showcard from the 1950s. Many of the advertisements of this time centred around sport and activity.

VIMTO-GLAZED HAM

SERVES 4-6

1 x 1.5–2kg gammon joint, skin on
6 black peppercorns
2 bay leaves
2 tablespoons demerara sugar
3 tablespoons Vimto squash
2 tablespoons honey
2 tablespoons dark muscovado sugar

Put the gammon joint into a large saucepan and cover with water. Add the peppercorns, bay leaves and demerara sugar and bring to the boil, then reduce the heat and simmer gently for 40 minutes.

Preheat the oven to 180°C/Gas Mark 4.

Lay out a sheet of foil, large enough to wrap the gammon. Carefully remove the gammon from the pan and place it in the centre of the foil, skin side up. Discard the remaining liquid in the pan. Wrap the gammon in the foil and place in a roasting tin, then pour in water to come 2.5cm up the sides of the tin. Cook in the centre of the oven for 1 hour.

Put the Vimto squash, honey and muscovado sugar into a small saucepan and bring to the boil. Lower the heat and simmer until it has reduced by half and become a syrupy liquid. Set aside.

Remove the gammon from the oven, carefully open the foil far enough to reveal the skin only, and drain off as much of the liquid as possible. Now cut off the skin, leaving the fat on the ham – it should peel off quite easily. Criss-cross the fat without cutting into the ham and brush the Vimto syrup all over the scored fat. Turn the oven up to 200°C/Gas Mark 6 and return the ham to the oven for about 20 minutes, brushing with more syrup a couple of times until the fat is golden.

Remove from the oven and allow to rest for 10 minutes. Now you can slice off delicious warm ham or leave it until cold to enjoy – or both!

VIMTO-BRAISED RED CABBAGE

SERVES 6

1 small whole red cabbage (about 600g)
1 tablespoon vegetable oil
1 medium onion, peeled and thinly sliced
300ml sparkling Vimto
50g butter
1 tablespoon lemon juice
½ teaspoon salt
freshly ground black pepper

Quarter the red cabbage and cut out the hard central core, then cut the cabbage into thin shreds.

Heat the vegetable oil in a large saucepan, add the onion and cook gently until transparent. Add the red cabbage, stir well, then turn the heat down to low and cook, covered, for 30 minutes.

Add the sparkling Vimto, butter, lemon juice, salt and pepper and stir well. Cover and cook slowly for a further 45 minutes, until the cabbage is tender. Remove the lid and cook until the juices have evaporated.

Perfect to serve with sausages and mash, game, casseroles, or anything that needs a vibrant, rich accompaniment.

a poem for
Faye
by Purple Ronnie

I've heard you think that Vimto's fab
And I can hardly disagree
So because you're all such massive fans
We've sent you some for free!

Vimto®
The fruitiest word I know

FIVE-SPICE PORK CHOPS WITH PLUM SAUCE

SERVES 2

1 teaspoon Chinese five-spice
2 free-range pork chops
sunflower oil, for frying
salt and freshly ground black pepper

FOR THE PLUM SAUCE

1 tablespoon olive oil
1 shallot, finely chopped
200g dark red plums, halved, stoned and cut into small wedges
50g demerara sugar
50ml Vimto squash
1 tablespoon Worcester sauce
300ml beef stock
1 star anise

Preheat the oven to 180°C/Gas Mark 4.

To make the sauce, heat the olive oil in a frying pan and cook the shallots until softened, then add the remaining sauce ingredients. Simmer for about 15 minutes, stirring occasionally until you have soft tender fruit. Leave aside to reheat when the chops are ready.

Sprinkle the five-spice over both sides of the pork chops and season well with salt and pepper. Heat a little oil in an oven-proof frying pan and add the chops. Cook on a fairly high heat for a few minutes each side to seal and brown the outside of the meat, then transfer to the oven for 8–10 minutes.

Allow the chops to rest for a few minutes, then serve on top of the fruity sauce.

STICKY PORK RIBS

SERVES 4

2kg pork spare ribs
1 heaped tablespoon barbecue spice mix
200g tomato ketchup
1 teaspoon chilli powder
2 tablespoons soy sauce
2 tablespoons teriyaki sauce
100g runny honey
2 tablespoons Vimto squash
4 tablespoons dry sherry

Heat the oven to 160°C/Gas Mark 3.

Put the pork ribs into a large dish and sprinkle the barbecue spice mix all over them. Rub the mix into the ribs with your hands. Lay the ribs out on a rack over a roasting tin, cover with foil and pop into the oven for 1 hour.

Put all the other ingredients into a heavy-based saucepan over a medium heat, mix well and simmer for 5 minutes. Remove from the heat.

Take the ribs from the oven, discard the foil and slather the sticky mixture all over them, turning to coat them on all sides. Pop back into the oven for 10 minutes, then remove, baste with the sticky glaze, and cook for a further 20 minutes.

Remove from the oven, rest for 5 minutes and serve.

a poem for
Maisie
by Purple Ronnie

If you want people to snog you
Then here's a word of advice
Swig a few mouthfuls of Vimto
Cause Vimto-ey kisses taste nice!

Vimto
The fruitiest word I know

The livery on the Vimto trucks over the years has seen more than a few changes. Above: replica lorries from years long gone; and right: the real thing in all its glory!

CRANBERRY SAUCE

MAKES 2 SMALL JARS

200g fresh cranberries
200g granulated sugar
½ teaspoon allspice
300ml Vimto squash
1 star anise

Put all the ingredients into a large saucepan, add 300ml of water, and simmer gently, stirring regularly, until all the fruits have softened and the mixture looks like jam. Remove from the heat and allow to cool a little.

Place two small glass jars (without lids) on a baking tray and pop them into a hot oven for 5 minutes to sterilise them. Spoon the mixture into the warm jars, and as soon as you are able to handle them, put the lids firmly on.

Label when cold and store until needed. The sauce keeps for 3 months in a sealed jar; once opened, keep it in the fridge.

LAMB CUTLETS WITH VIMTO AND ROSEMARY GRAVY

SERVES 4

oil, for frying
4 English lamb cutlets
a knob of butter
1 teaspoon flour
a good glug of red wine
300ml good beef stock
2 tablespoons Vimto squash
1 sprig of fresh rosemary
salt and freshly ground black pepper

Heat a little oil in a large frying pan, then season the cutlets on both sides and add to the pan. Cook over a high heat for 3–4 minutes on each side, then reduce the heat to low and cook for a further 8–10 minutes, until cooked to your liking. When done, remove the lamb from the pan and keep warm.

Add the butter to the pan and quickly stir in the flour to make a roux, using any juices left in the pan. Add the wine, stock, Vimto squash and rosemary and stir well. Simmer for 5 minutes, then strain into a jug to remove the rosemary stalks. Serve the gravy over the lamb chops, with your favourite vegetables.

TOP SECRET!

Vimto has a top-secret unique recipe that has changed little from Noel Nichols' original creation. Only four people know the full list of approximately 29 ingredients and their proportions! We do know that the list includes grape, blackcurrant and raspberry juices, along with a mysterious blend of 23 fruit essences, herbs and spices. Only the very best ingredients are used to ensure that Vimto tastes totally terrific.

PAN-FRIED DUCK BREAST WITH CRIMSON SAUCE

SERVES 4

4 duck breasts, skin on
150g chopped shallots
2 tablespoons Vimto squash
2 tablespoons red wine vinegar
1 teaspoon pink peppercorns
juice and zest of 2 medium oranges

Prepare the duck breasts by scoring the skin with a sharp knife twice each way diagonally (do not cut through the meat). Put a heavy-based frying pan on a medium heat and when hot add the duck breasts, skin side down. Cook for 3–4 minutes, then turn the heat down to low and continue cooking for about 10 minutes, until the skin is golden and crispy.

Turn the duck breasts and cook for a further 4–5 minutes, depending on how pink you like your duck. Tip the duck fat into a bowl, keeping any left over to use for your roast potatoes next time, and leave the duck breasts to rest in a warm place while you make the sauce.

Pour 2 tablespoons of the fat back into the pan and sauté the shallots until softened but not brown. Stir in the remaining ingredients and simmer until reduced to a rich sauce. Season with salt and pepper and serve with the duck breasts.

PIGEON BREASTS WITH VIMTO COULIS

SERVES 2

8 pigeon breasts
vegetable oil, for frying
dressed salad leaves, to serve
salt and freshly ground black pepper

FOR THE VIMTO COULIS
3 tablespoons Vimto squash
2 tablespoons port
2 tablespoons balsamic vinegar

Season the pigeon breasts on both sides. Heat a little oil in a frying pan, add the breasts, and cook for 3–4 minutes on each side, longer if you don't like your pigeon pink. Set aside to rest and keep warm.

Put the Vimto squash, port and balsamic vinegar into a small saucepan and bring to the boil. Season well with salt and a good grind of black pepper, then simmer until thickened and reduced by about half.

Pile some salad leaves in the centre of two plates. Slice each pigeon breast three or four times lengthways, arrange the slices in a fan shape around the leaves and drizzle the coulis over.

VIMTO'S GONNA GET'CHA IN THE END!

This advertising campaign from the 1980s featured Derek Griffiths, one of children's TV's favourite entertainers from the day. The advert centred around the mysterious ingredients which make up Vimto's unique taste. Griffiths would finish with the catchphrase, 'Vimto's gonna get'cha in the end.'

GUINEA FOWL JACKETS WITH VIMTO AND REDCURRANT SAUCE

SERVES 8

8 small jacket potatoes
olive oil
2 guinea fowl
8 rashers of streaky bacon
50g butter
1 carrot, finely diced
1 medium onion, finely diced
2 sticks of celery, finely diced
700ml chicken stock
a 2.5cm piece of fresh ginger, finely chopped
50ml Vimto squash
100ml medium sherry
60g plain flour
1 tablespoon tomato purée
150g redcurrants
salt and freshly ground black pepper

Preheat the oven to 180°C/Gas Mark 6.

Put the potatoes into a roasting tin, coat with olive oil and sprinkle with plenty of salt. Place at the bottom of the oven and cook for 1 hour.

Clean the guinea fowl, season inside and out with salt and pepper, and cover the breasts with the bacon. Melt the butter in a roasting tin on the hob and add the carrots, onion and celery (a classic mirepoix). Cook over a gentle heat for 5 minutes. Sit the birds on top, add a splash of stock and pop them into the oven for 45–50 minutes.

When cooked, lift the birds out of the pan to rest and keep warm. Carefully put the roasting tin back on the hob, add the ginger, Vimto squash, sherry, flour, tomato purée and the rest of the stock, and stir together well. Cook for 10 minutes, stirring, over a medium heat, then strain into a saucepan. Add the redcurrants, reserving a few for garnish, and poach for a few minutes.

Put a jacket potato on each plate, cut a cross in the top and squeeze open. Cut the guinea fowl into joints and arrange alongside each jacket, then drizzle over the sauce and top with a few extra redcurrants. A wonderful winter warmer.

Vimto is sold across the globe, with tweaks to the base recipe applied here and there to suit the tastes of some territories. In Africa, it is fantastically popular and is available across 30 different countries.

VENISON WITH VIMTO AND GIN

SERVES 4

4 venison steaks, 150–200g each
50ml gin
30ml Vimto squash
a splash of vegetable oil, for frying
200ml good beef stock
1 tablespoon redcurrant jelly
salt and freshly ground black pepper

Put the venison steaks into a shallow dish. Mix together the gin and Vimto squash, pour over the steaks, then leave to marinate for an hour, turning them a few times. Keep the marinade to use later.

Season the steaks on both sides with salt and pepper. Heat the oil in a heavy-based frying pan and seal the venison on both sides over a high heat. Turn down to a low heat and cook for 5 minutes on each side, longer if you don't want your meat pink. Set the venison aside to keep warm and allow it to rest while you make the sauce.

Add the Vimto marinade and stock to the frying pan and bring to the boil. Stir in the redcurrant jelly and keep simmering until the sauce is reduced to the consistency of thick gravy.

Pour the sauce over the venison steaks and serve.

LIVER WITH VIMTO BALSAMIC GLAZE

SERVES 4

600g lambs' liver, sliced
olive oil, for cooking
1 x 400g tin of Puy or green lentils
50ml Vimto squash
50ml balsamic vinegar
salt and freshly ground black pepper

Sprinkle salt and plenty of black pepper on both sides of each slice of liver.

Heat a frying pan and add a little oil. Now add the liver, cooking it on each side for 3–4 minutes, depending on the thickness of the slices. When cooked to your liking, remove from the pan to rest and keep warm.

Drain the lentils, rinse thoroughly and cook in lightly salted boiling water for 5 minutes.

Put the frying pan back on a high heat, add the Vimto squash and balsamic vinegar and cook until reduced by half and syrupy.

Serve the liver on top of the drained lentils, with the sauce drizzled over.

A LITTLE KNOWLEDGE

The Vimto Book of Knowledge was published regularly throughout the early to mid-20th century. It was a trivia book to aid self-improvement. Vimto founder, Noel Nichols, was a great believer in self-instruction and so the book was very much in line with this ethos.

A showcard from the mid-1920s, illustrating that Vimto added *vim to* your day.

VIMTO MUFFINS

MAKES 12

250g self-raising flour
25g ground almonds
½ teaspoon bicarbonate of soda
75g caster sugar
1 teaspoon baking powder
200ml Vimto squash
6 drops of red food colouring
100ml milk
75g butter, melted and left to cool
1 egg, beaten

FOR THE TOPPING

200g icing sugar
100g mascarpone cheese
25ml Vimto squash

Preheat the oven to 180°C/Gas Mark 4.

Put the flour, ground almonds, bicarbonate of soda, caster sugar and baking powder into a large bowl and mix together.

Combine the Vimto squash, food colouring, milk, butter and egg in another bowl and add to the dry ingredients, mixing very, very gently. Do not over-mix.

Pour into 12 muffin cases or a greased muffin tin, filling each case to approximately halfway, and cook in the centre of the oven for 15 minutes.

Turn out on to a rack and leave to cool.

Mix the topping ingredients in a large bowl. Dip the tops of the cooled muffins into the topping and leave to set.

CUPCAKES WITH VIMTO BUTTER CREAM

MAKES 12

FOR THE CUPCAKES
150g butter
150g caster sugar
3 eggs, beaten
150g self-raising flour

FOR THE BUTTERCREAM
75g butter
150g icing sugar
30ml Vimto squash

Preheat the oven to 180°C/Gas Mark 4.

Cream the butter and caster sugar together in a large bowl until light and fluffy. Gradually add the beaten eggs, beating the mixture after each addition. Sift the flour into the mixture and fold in.

Divide the mixture between twelve cupcake cases and bake for 12–15 minutes, or until a skewer comes out cleanly. When ready, turn out on to a wire rack and leave to cool.

To make the topping, cream the butter and icing sugar together until light and fluffy and add Vimto squash to taste. Pipe the buttercream on top of the cooled cakes and decorate with whatever your heart desires. Cupcakes are so popular you can choose from a myriad of wonderful sprinkles for any occasion.

INTRODUCING...
VIMTOAD!

Vimtoad follows on from the 3 fruit in Vimto's 'Seriously Mixed Up Fruit' campaign – broadening the appeal of the brand to mums.

VIMTO FRUIT TERRINE

SERVES 8

10 sheets of leaf gelatine
300ml sparkling Vimto
100ml Vimto squash
1 large ripe mango (or 2 small), peeled and
    sliced
350g whole raspberries
250g whole blueberries
350g strawberries, sliced
fresh mint leaves, to garnish

You will need a terrine dish or a 450g loaf tin.

Soak the gelatine leaves in cold water until they become very soft and slippery (this takes about 10 minutes).

Line the terrine dish with clingfilm and pop it into the freezer while you prepare the fruit. This will help the jelly set quicker.

Warm the sparkling Vimto and squash in a saucepan, and when just steaming remove from the heat and slide in the gelatine leaves, one at a time. Set aside.

Using a star or suitable shaped cutter, cut three emblems out of the sliced mango. Place the emblems in the bottom of the dish and cover with raspberries, making sure you get them along all the sides and into the corners. Ladle in about half of the Vimto jelly mixture to just cover the fruit. Now add the remaining slices of mango, then blueberries, then strawberries, and finally another layer of mango. Ladle in the rest of the Vimto jelly mix until the fruit is covered again. Cover with clingfilm and weight it all down with a couple of tins from the store cupboard.

Place on a tray and chill for 24 hours. Remove the top clingfilm, turn out, remove the rest of the clingfilm and serve in gorgeously coloured layered slices, with a leaf of fresh mint.

FROZEN BERRY YOGURT

SERVES 6

100g fresh blueberries
500g natural Greek yoghurt
100ml Vimto squash
2 tablespoons runny honey
1 x 450g pack of frozen mixed berries
sprigs of fresh mint, to garnish

Divide the fresh blueberries between six glasses.

Put the yoghurt, Vimto squash and honey into a blender and blitz until mixed. Add the frozen berries and blitz again.

Spoon the yoghurt over the blueberries, add a sprig of mint to each glass and serve with long spoons.

Vimto ®
as drunk by Purple Ronnie
The fruitiest word I know

TEAMING UP WITH ANOTHER PURPLE ICON!

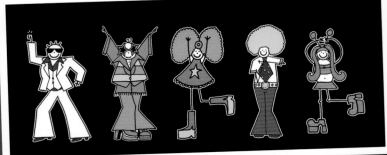

In the 1990s, Vimto teamed up with Purple Ronnie®, giving their marketing a vibrant – not to mention very purple – new facelift. The team-up was a great success and covered campaigns both in print and on television. Here are some of the colourful characters that were part of the campaign!

THE
SKY'S
THE
LIMIT

SERIOUSLY
MIXED UP FRUIT

VIMTO AND BLACKCURRANT ICE CREAM

SERVES 6-8

**400g blackcurrants, fresh or frozen and
 defrosted with juice retained
180g caster sugar
150ml Vimto squash
275ml double cream**

Put the berries, in two or three batches, into a sieve over a bowl. Press hard on the berries with the back of a spoon to extract all the juice and fruit, leaving behind the stalks, pips and skin.

Put the sugar, Vimto squash and 50ml of water into a small saucepan and heat until the sugar is completely dissolved. Boil for 2–3 minutes, then remove from the heat and stir into the fruit juices.

Whip the cream until it begins to thicken – not too much. Fold the cream into the blackcurrant mixture and mix together well. Tip into a plastic container and pop into the freezer for 2 hours, until the ice cream begins to set.

Bring it out of the freezer, tip it into a bowl and beat it really well. This will prevent crystals forming in the ice cream. Repeat this process twice more and the ice cream will be ready.

Take your ice cream out of the freezer and put it into the fridge at least half an hour before you want to eat it.

ALL MIXED UP!

Vimto's 'Seriously Mixed Up Fruit' campaign was launched with the 3 fruit characters, opposite, who went out of their way (very far out of their way!) to get themselves all mixed up into delicious Vimto.

GIN, CHERRY VIMTO AND POMEGRANATE GRANITA

SERVES 6-8

½ a pomegranate
400ml soda water or tonic water
200ml cherry Vimto squash
50ml gin

Mix the soda or tonic water, cherry Vimto squash and gin together in a flat plastic tub or container – the flatter it is, the better. Place in the freezer until crystals have started to form (about 4 hours or overnight).

Remove the container from the freezer and gently scrape the surface of the frozen liquid to create crystals. Put back into the freezer. Repeat this process until it is all crystallised, at which point your granita is ready to eat.

Take the seeds out of the pomegranate by bashing the skin while holding the cut surface over a bowl. Mix in the pomegranate seeds, scoop into a glass and serve. You can also drizzle over some Vimto ice cream topping, if you like.

DOUBLE WHAMMY

Double-strength Vimto is very popular in Muslim countries, especially during Ramadan. The extra sweetness and 'kick' is a great restorer of energy after a day of fasting.

VIMTO TRIFLE

SERVES 8-10

FOR THE JELLY
5 leaves of gelatine
300ml Vimto squash
1 pack of 12 trifle sponges

FOR THE CUSTARD
300ml milk
300ml double cream
6 drops of red food colouring
100ml Vimto squash
2 egg yolks

FOR THE TOPPING
600ml double cream
2 teaspoons caster sugar
grated chocolate or hundreds and thousands,
    for decoration

Soak the gelatine in cold water for 10 minutes.

Put the Vimto squash into a saucepan with 300ml of cold water and heat until warm. Add the gelatine, a leaf at a time, and stir until it has dissolved. Do not allow to boil. Set aside until it has cooled but not set.

Arrange the trifle sponges in the bottom of your trifle dish and pour over the cooled jelly mixture. Put into the fridge and leave to set for up to 24 hours.

To make the custard, put the milk, cream, food colouring and Vimto squash into a saucepan and heat gently, but do not allow to boil. Whisk the egg yolks in a large bowl.

Pour a small amount of the warmed milk mixture over the eggs, stirring constantly. Pour the eggs back into the milk pan and bring to the boil, then reduce the heat to a simmer for 5–6 minutes. Set aside to cool.

Once the custard has cooled, spoon it on top of the cooled jelly. Whisk the cream and caster sugar gently until soft peaks form, and spoon on top of the custard.

Decorate with grated chocolate or hundreds and thousands.

SUMMER PUDDING

SERVES 4-6

400g mixed berries (e.g. strawberries, raspberries, blackberries, blackcurrants), fresh, or frozen and defrosted with juice retained
1 tablespoon caster sugar
200ml Vimto squash
5 medium slices of white bread, crusts removed

You will need a 500ml pudding bowl or similar domed dish.

Put the berries into a dish and add the sugar and Vimto squash. Set aside to steep for half an hour. Drain the fruit and put the juices into a shallow dish.

Reserving one slice for the top, dip the slices of bread into the juices, one at a time, and mould them all round the base and inside of the pudding bowl, filling in any gaps. Fill the centre with the fruit, then cut a circle from the other piece of bread, dipped in the juices, to fit the top of the bowl – it should reach right to the edge. If you run out of juice for dipping, don't worry – it will seep from the fruit later. Cover with clingfilm and chill.

After 2 hours, remove the clingfilm and turn the pudding over on to a rimmed plate (the rim will catch any excess juice), leaving the bowl on top until you want to serve it. This will make sure the base is full of juice and the pudding keeps its shape.

Remove the bowl and serve at room temperature, cut in wedges, with a good dollop of clotted cream.

VIMTO AND APPLE CRUMBLE

SERVES 6

25g butter
1kg cooking apples, peeled, cored and sliced
500ml sparkling Vimto
50ml Vimto squash
2 tablespoons granulated sugar

FOR THE CRUMBLE TOPPING

200g flour
150g butter, cut into small cubes
½ pack of digestive biscuits
4 tablespoons demerara sugar
3 tablespoons porridge oats

Preheat the oven to 180°C/Gas Mark 4.

Melt the butter in a large saucepan and add the apples. Turn them in the butter, then add the sparkling Vimto, Vimto squash and granulated sugar and cook until just softened. Lift out the apples with a slotted spoon into an ovenproof dish, leaving any excess juice behind. Set aside while you prepare the crumble topping.

Put the flour and butter into a food processor and blitz until you have a crumb consistency. Break up the digestive biscuits, add to the processor and pulse until they are broken down. Tip the lot into a bowl and add the demerara sugar and oats. Stir to mix everything together.

Sprinkle the mixture over the apples without pressing down at all. Place the dish on an oven tray in case the juices overspill while cooking, and put into the centre of the oven. Bake for 30 minutes, or until the crumble topping is golden and crunchy.

Serve warm, with lashings of custard or extra thick double cream.

VIMTO AND CHERRY CHEESECAKE

**SERVES 10-12
(WILL KEEP CHILLED FOR 5 DAYS)**

125g digestive biscuits
75g gingernut biscuits
120g melted butter
600g condensed milk
350ml fresh double cream
100ml Vimto squash
50ml lemon juice
zest of 1 lemon
a handful of black cherries (fresh or tinned),
    halved

You will need a 30cm flan tin (ideally fluted) with a removable base.

Put all the biscuits into a blender and blitz until crumbed. Gradually add the melted butter and mix. Tip the biscuit mix into a buttered flan tin and gently press to cover the base, pushing into the fluted edges if using this type of tin. Pop into the freezer while you make the topping.

Put the condensed milk and double cream into a perfectly clean, dry mixing bowl and mix, using an electric whisk, until you have a slightly stiff, creamy mixture – this may take a few minutes. Add the Vimto squash, lemon juice and zest and mix briefly to combine.

Remove the biscuit base from the freezer and tip the creamy mixture all over the base, finishing with a spatula for a nice even finish right up to the edges of the tin. Pop into the fridge and leave for at least 4 hours, or ideally overnight.

Remove from the tin and scatter with the halved black cherries – yummy!

A WHOLE LOTTA VIMTO!

Millions of people love the fruity flavour of Vimto in all its forms. Each year, Vimto sells more than 12 million bottles of Vimto squash, and 26 million bottles and 92 million cans of fizzy Vimto in the UK alone. There are more than 30 different types of different Vimto products you can find in the shops, from bon bons to jelly and from ice lollies to candy floss!

PEARS POACHED IN VIMTO

SERVES 4

4 Conference pears
300ml Vimto squash
ice cream, to serve

Peel the pears with a vegetable peeler, being careful to leave the stalk in the top and keeping the pear a nice shape. Cut the bottom off each pear so that the base is flat and it will stand upright. Remove the core of each pear from the base upwards, leaving the stalk in place.

Put the Vimto squash into a saucepan with 300ml of water and bring to the boil. Reduce to a simmer and carefully place the pears on their sides in the pan. Cook for about 20 minutes, until tender, turning them regularly.

When cooked, remove the pears from the pan and keep warm. Boil the remaining liquid until thick and syrupy.

Serve the pears with a scoop of vanilla ice cream alongside and the syrup poured over the top.

BANANA FRITTERS

SERVES 4

200g plain flour
100g cornflour
1 teaspoon baking powder
350ml sparkling Vimto
50ml Vimto squash
1 teaspoon sesame oil
4 bananas
sunflower oil, for frying
caster sugar
vanilla ice cream, to serve

Sift the flour, cornflour and baking powder into a bowl, then add the sparkling Vimto, Vimto squash and sesame oil. Mix well with a wooden spoon until you have a smooth batter.

Cut the bananas in half, then in half again lengthways. Put them into the batter and turn to coat.

Half fill a deep heavy-based saucepan with oil and heat it until a cube of bread sizzles when you drop it in. Using kitchen tongs, carefully lower each piece of banana into the hot oil – you will need to cook them in two batches. Deep-fry for about 3–4 minutes, or until golden. Lift out with a slotted spoon and place on kitchen paper to drain.

Sprinkle with caster sugar and serve warm, with vanilla ice cream.

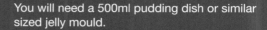

VIMTO JELLY WITH FROSTED GRAPES

SERVES 4-6

6 leaves of gelatine
150ml Vimto squash
350–400g mixed black and white grapes,
    cut into 4–6 bunches
1 egg white
3 tablespoons caster sugar

You will need a 500ml pudding dish or similar sized jelly mould.

Soak the gelatine leaves in cold water for 10 minutes.

Put the Vimto squash into a saucepan with 350ml of water and heat gently. Add the gelatine, one leaf at a time, until completely dissolved. Remove from the heat, allow to cool a little, then pour into the bowl or jelly mould. When completely cold, pop into the fridge to set.

Wash and pat dry the bunches of grapes and lay out on some kitchen paper. Beat the egg white with 1 teaspoon of water and paint it all over the grapes, using a pastry brush. Sprinkle the grapes with the caster sugar and set aside to dry.

Serve the scrummy Vimto jelly with the frosted bunches of grapes. Perfect for kids of all ages.

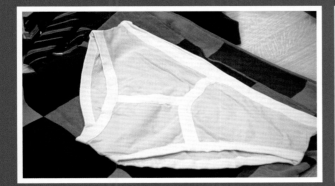

DAD'S PANTS!

In 2006, Vimto launched an all-new and all-fun TV commercial – 'Dad's Pants'. It was the story of Billy, who turns up at the swimming pool with his Dad's pants sandwiched in the middle of his rolled-up towel, instead of his swimming trunks. After a quick schlurp on his beloved Vimto, Billy cleverly and cutely manages to turn misfortune into a stunt that wins the admiration of the rest of his class. The 'Dad's Pants' theme tune went on to become something of a cult song around the country's school playgrounds!

VIMTO AND PLUM FOOL

SERVES 6

600g plums, halved, stoned and quartered
100g caster sugar
150ml Vimto squash
1 tablespoon plum brandy
275ml double cream
sprigs of fresh mint, to serve

Put the plums, sugar and Vimto squash into a saucepan and cook gently for about 15 minutes, stirring occasionally, until the plums are lovely and soft.

Pop the plums into a blender and blitz to a purée. Transfer to a bowl, add the plum brandy and leave to cool.

In a separate bowl, whisk the double cream until it forms soft peaks. Fold this into the plum purée, a little at a time. Chill until ready to serve.

Spoon into wine glasses and finish with sprigs of mint.

CENTENARY CAPERS

A special edition of the board game Cluedo was created as part of the Vimto centenary celebrations. Instead of a murderer, players had to identify the person who stole the special Vimto centenary birthday cake from the factory. Twists on the standard cast included Colonel Cordial, Fizzy Lizzy, Professor Purple, Sidney Shlurpler, Bella Beverage and Miss Redgrape.

VIMTO CURD

150g butter
250ml Vimto squash
2 teaspoons caster sugar
a pinch of salt
1 egg

Put the butter, Vimto squash, sugar, salt and 1 teaspoon of cold water into a heatproof bowl and stir gently over a pan of simmering water, being careful not to let the bowl touch the water.

When the sugar has dissolved, whisk in the egg and continue to heat, whisking constantly. When the mixture has thickened to the consistency of custard, remove from the heat and allow to cool. If you like your curd a bit less sweet, add a little lemon juice to taste.

Spread on toast, or use like any other kind of curd or jam. It will keep in a jar in the fridge for up to 7 days.

A 100th birthday means a telegram from the Queen. And so it was with Vimto's special birthday... well, almost! This lookalikey Queen met with John Nichols, the Chairman of Nichols Plc, to present him with a birthday telegram and to mark 100 amazing years since the brand was created by Nichols' grandfather, Noel.

THE SEQUELCH

The classic lowrider car which featured in the iconic advertising campaign from 2011. It was an instant hit and even spawned a chart-topping hit, 'Bounce 'n' Boom'. And that was just the beginning of a cross-platform campaign which even saw Vimto becoming the first ever brand to take over the MTV website.

VIMTO MERINGUE PIE

SERVES 6

FOR THE PASTRY
225g plain flour
175g cold butter, cubed
45g caster sugar
1 large free-range egg, beaten

FOR THE VIMTO CURD
see recipe on page 69

FOR THE MERINGUE
4 free-range egg whites
225g caster sugar
2 teaspoons cornflour

You will need a 23cm loose-based flan tin.

Put the flour and butter into a food processor and blitz until you have fine crumbs. Add the sugar, egg and 1 tablespoon of cold water and process until you have a ball of pastry. Roll it out on a floured surface and mould into the tin, leaving an overlap all round. Chill in the fridge for 10 minutes.

Preheat the oven to 190°C/Gas 5. Prick the base of the pastry with a fork, line with baking paper and fill with baking beans. Bake in the oven for 15 minutes, then remove the paper and beans and return it to the oven for 5 minutes.

Remove from the oven and place the tin on a rack to cool. Turn the oven down to 170°C/Gas Mark 3.

For the meringue, whisk the egg whites until soft peaks form when the whisk is removed. Add the sugar a little at a time, still whisking until the meringue is stiff and glossy. Add the cornflour and whisk again.

Trim the excess pastry from the tin and spread the Vimto curd all over the base. Spoon the meringue on top, spreading it all over and lifting the spoon upwards to create peaks. Bake in the centre of the oven for 15 minutes, or until the top of the meringue is lightly golden and crisp.

Serve warm or cold.

CHERRY VIMTO TARTE

SERVES 6-8

FOR THE PASTRY
150g cold butter, cubed
200g plain flour
a pinch of salt
45g caster sugar
1 egg, beaten

FOR THE FILLING
200ml double cream
125g dark chocolate (70% cocoa works best)
50g milk chocolate
150ml cherry Vimto squash
cocoa powder, for dusting
crushed hazelnuts (optional)

You will need a buttered 25cm loose-based flan tin.

Preheat the oven to 180°C/Gas Mark 4.

Put the butter and flour into a food processor and blend until you have fine breadcrumbs. Add the salt, sugar, egg and 2 teaspoons of cold water and mix again until the pastry forms a ball.

Roll out the pastry on a floured surface, then mould it into the flan tin. Prick the base with a fork, line with baking paper and fill with baking beans.

Bake in the centre of the oven for 15 minutes, then remove the paper and bake for a further 10 minutes, until fully cooked. Remove from the oven and set aside to cool.

To make the filling, put the cream, chocolates and cherry Vimto squash into a heatproof bowl set over a pan of simmering water and allow to melt completely. Do not let the bowl touch the water. Remove from the heat and leave to cool.

Pour the cooled mixture into the pastry case and pop it into the fridge to set. Just before serving, dust with the cocoa powder and sprinkle over the hazelnuts, if using.

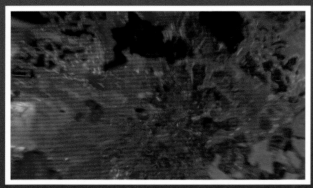

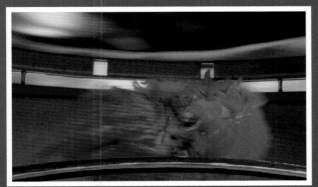

SERIOUSLY MIXED UP FRUIT

In 2009, we were introduced to anthropomorphic incarnations of the fruits which make up Vimto. Raspberry, grape and blackcurrant characters worked their way into scenarios which would see them 'seriously mixed up' by the advert's end.

RED ONION MARMALADE

MAKES 3 OR 4 SMALL JARS

1 tablespoon vegetable oil
1kg red onions, peeled and sliced into
  half-moons
50ml Vimto squash
2 tablespoons brown sugar
2 tablespoons red wine vinegar
salt and freshly ground black pepper

Heat the vegetable oil in a large heavy-based saucepan. Add the onions, and when they start to cook turn the heat down to low and pop a lid on. Cook for half an hour, stirring occasionally, or until the onions are really soft.

Add the Vimto squash, sugar and red wine vinegar and season with salt and pepper. Cook for a further 15 minutes, or until all the liquid has evaporated. Check the taste now – if you like it a little sweeter add more sugar, and if you like it more tart add more red wine vinegar.

Put two glass jars (without lids) on to a baking tray and pop them into a hot oven for 5 minutes to sterilise them. Carefully ladle the onion marmalade into the warm jars, and as soon as you are able to handle them, pop the lids on and leave to cool. This should keep in the fridge for a couple of months.

VIMTO ROYALE COCKTAIL

PER PERSON

2 parts sparkling Vimto
5 parts Champagne or good Cava
1 part cherry brandy
a dash of fresh lemon juice
caster sugar, for dipping
fresh cherries on their stems, or
 glacé cherrie

Mix all the ingredients together in a jug and chill.

Take a champagne flute and turn it upside down. Dip the rim into 5ml of cold water and then into 5ml of caster sugar. Turn the glass the right way up and carefully drop in a cherry. Stir well, then pour the mixture from the jug into the glass, up to just under the sugar line, and sip away.

INTO THE FUTURE...

Over the last few years, Vimto has grown and grown and as the aisles brim with fantastic-tasting products, Vimto's charm has extended into the online world too, with a fully interactive website. You can play the Bounce 'n' Boom game or share your love of the purple stuff at the Vimto Facebook page. And while there, you can ponder on what the future holds... Vimto-flavoured popcorn, Vimto-flavoured cereal, Vimto water fountains and, er... a slightly different take on purple-sprouting broccoli!

ACKNOWLEDGEMENTS

The idea for this book came on a Sunday afternoon several years ago while making apple crumble. As always, there was some Vimto in the cupboard and I just decided to add a splash. I was hooked!

After the success of that, I tried a few other things such as poached pears and the cranberry sauce and decided there and then to write the book.

We have all heard the stories of struggling authors trying to get something published and this is no exception.

Little did I know that there was a man out there with a wealth of knowledge and a generous nature who would be the one to make this happen.

Paul Hartley is the author of a complete series of brand cookbooks and, without him, this book would never have got off the ground. I owe Paul a great debt of gratitude for making my 'silly idea' a reality. Thank you to Paul and, of course, his lovely wife, Lynda. You made my dream come true.

Another enormous thank you goes to James Nichols at Nichols Plc, the owners of Vimto, for his co-operation and enthusiasm. It's not every marketing department that is prepared to commit to an idea like this, so my gratitude goes out to them.

The team at Absolute Press and Bloomsbury also deserve special mention: Jon Croft for agreeing to the idea in the first place; Alice Gibbs for all her help in co-ordinating every minute detail; and Matt Inwood for making everything look so fantastic. Thank you all for your efforts.

I also have to make a special mention to my family for putting up with all the hours of work that have had to go into creating this book and for making short work of all the failed attempts of getting the recipes right. My children, Robert and Grace, have enjoyed every minute of this project and I have been supported tremendously by my loving wife, Dee-Ann. Thank you all so much....

DAVID CLARE

The publishers would like to thank Nichols Plc for their help in collating the materials in this book and for allowing their reproduction. This book is produced under licence from Nichols plc, WA12 0HH, UK, owner of the registered trademark Vimto®. Purple Ronnie® is a registered trademark of Purple Enterprises Limited. More information regarding the history of Vimto can be found in *Vimto: The Story of a Soft Drink*, by Sue Nichols.